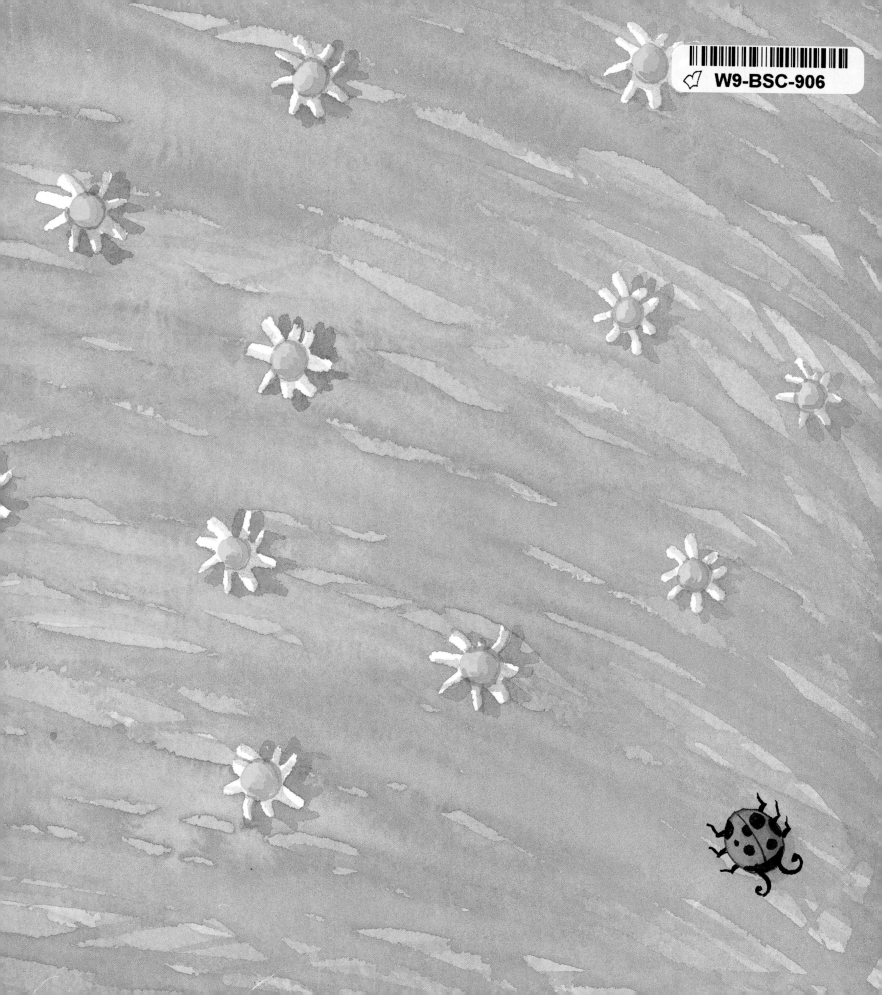

For my daughters —
in amazement and with love.
— D.G.

Library of Congress Cataloging-in-Publication Data available.

ISBN 0-439-45590-1

10 9 8 7 6 5 4 3 2   03 04 05 06 07

Printed in Dubai
First Scholastic edition, March 2003
Reinforced binding for library use

The text was set in LombaMedium.
The display type was set in Maiandra Demi Bold.

Flora's Surprise!

Debi Gliori

Orchard Books

AN IMPRINT OF SCHOLASTIC INC.

NEW YORK

Flora's family loved their garden.

Norah planted a huge amaryllis.
Cora planted twenty pink tulips.

"Be careful, Flora," said her sisters.

Sam planted lettuce,

Tom planted sunflowers,

and Max sprinkled alfalfa seeds
on a wet towel.

"Don't touch, Flora,"
said her brothers.

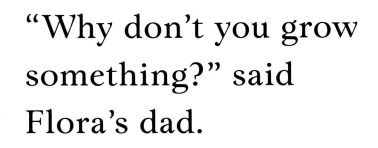

"Why don't you grow something?" said Flora's dad.

"Some pretty flowers?" said Flora's mom.
Flora planted a small brick.
"I'm growing a house," said Flora.

"Your brick won't grow as quickly as my alfalfa sprouts," said Max.

"Or as well as my lettuce," said Sam.

"Or as tall as my sunflowers," said Tom.
"It's not a brick, it's a house," said Flora.

Up sprang Cora's tulips, and
Norah's amaryllis grew and
grew and grew. . . .

"How's your brick, Flora?" asked Norah and Cora.
"It's not a brick, it's a house," muttered Flora.

Every night for a week, they ate Sam's lettuce with a garnish of Max's sprouts.

"How's your brick, Flora?" asked Tom.
"It's not a brick, it's a house," sniffed Flora.

Norah's amaryllis burst open and Cora's tulips were beautiful.

Flora poked
at her house
hopefully.

Flora put her house outside, beside Tom's spectacular sunflowers, but still nothing happened.

"I think your brick is dead," said Sam.

"It's NOT a BRICK!" wailed Flora. "IT'S A HOUSE!"

Winter came, and snow fell.
Nothing grew — inside or out.

Then, one day, spring came back, and
Flora's family emerged from their burrow.

"LOOK!" yelled Flora. "MY HOUSE!"
For Flora's brick had grown . . .

. . . into a perfect house.

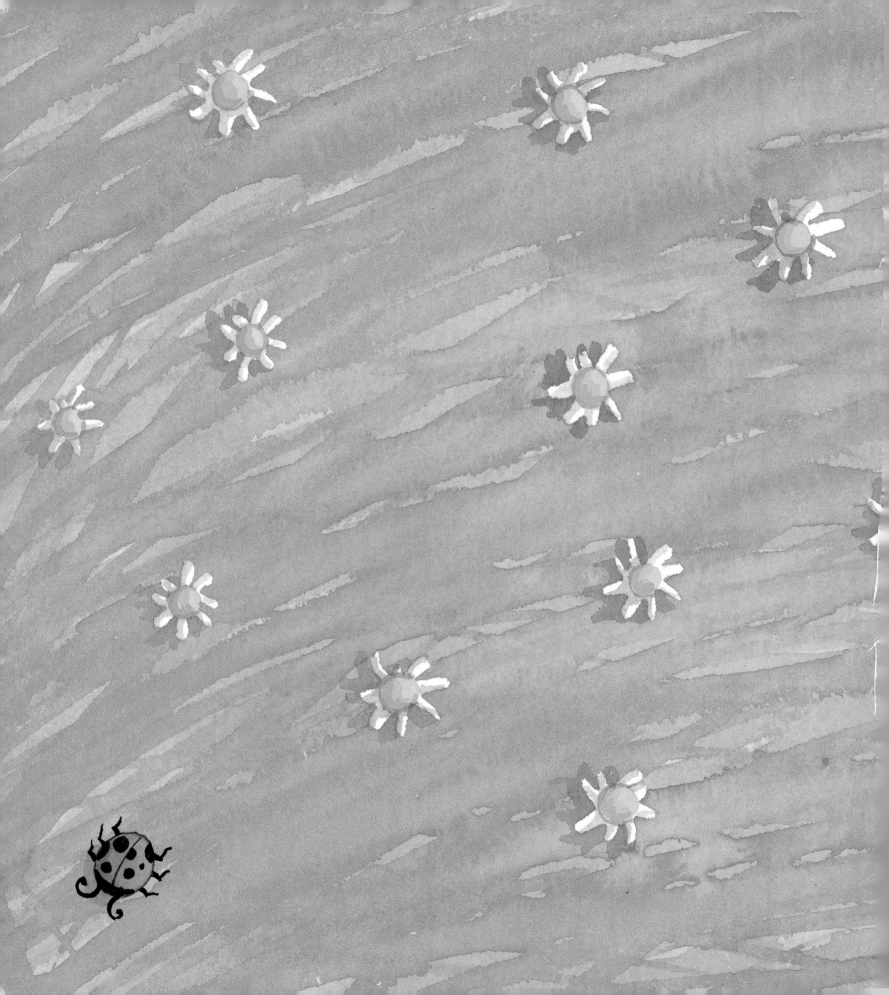